FUN S
TRICKS FOR
BEGINNERS

A Workbook
of Slalom Basics

Skater Name: _____

Age: _____

Start Date: _____

by Naomi Grigg

FUN SKATE TRICKS FOR BEGINNERS
A Workbook of Slalom Basics

ISBN-13: 978-1723306952
ISBN-10: 1723306959

 Patson Media
San Francisco

Also by Naomi Grigg:

The Art of Falling: Freestyle Slalom Skating

Contents

*Parent/Instructor
Score Sheet
follows Trick 4*

*Parent/Instructor
Score Sheet
follows Trick 7*

*Parent/Instructor
Score Sheet
follows Trick 12*

*Parent/Instructor
Score Sheet
follows Trick 17*

*Parent/Instructor
Score Sheet
follows Trick 20*

Getting Started

Here are some tips for using this book:

It's for total beginner skaters!

This book is for complete beginner skaters and is intended to help beginner skaters to have fun on their skates. Even adult beginners!

It's for ALL types of skating!

The tricks in this book develop skills for slalom and many other types of skating including just having fun in the park. It's about having fun on skates and wanting to skate more and more.

Write in it!

It's a workbook so you can write in it! Mark on the page each time you try a trick, color the pictures, and at the end of each section there is a score sheet for parents or adult instructors to help chart the skater's progress.

Fun not Perfection!

The most important thing to remember when trying these tricks is that having fun by trying and experimenting is much more important than being able to do them perfectly.

Trying counts!

Have a go at the tricks even if you don't think you'll be able to do them or do them well. It is the having-a-go that will have your skating becoming easier. Just keep doing it and you'll get better and better...and you'll have fun!

Getting Started
YOUR SKATES

There are two main types of skates: Inline skates and roller skates. Inline skates are sometimes called 'rollerblades', and roller skates are also called 'quad skates'.

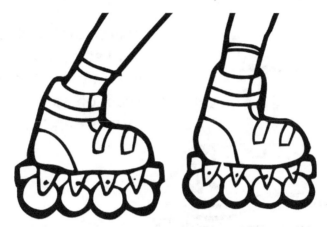

Inline skates have all of their wheels in a line, so they can be easier to balance on and move faster.

Roller skates have their wheels in the four corners of each skate which makes it easier to stand on one foot.

Getting Started
HEEL BRAKES & TOE STOPS

New skates usually have brakes on them. Inlines have 'heel brakes' on the right foot, and roller skates have 'toe stoppers' on both toes.

Inlines:

When you are comfortable with turning and stopping on your skates without using the brake, you can take it off so that you can do more tricks on your skates.

Quads:

When you are comfortable with turning and stopping on your skates without using the toe stops, you can replace them with smaller "plugs."

Getting Started
WHEELS FOR TRICKS

Your skates will come with **8** wheels that are the same size

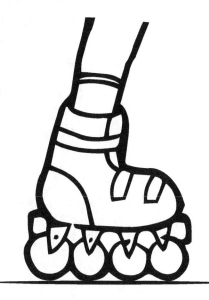

If you are using inline skates, you can make them easier to do tricks in by replacing the front and back wheels with slightly smaller ones.

Your feet will feel like they are in rocking chairs which is a shock at the beginning, but you'll soon get used to it and the tricks in this book will become much easier!

SAFETY GEAR: HELMET

You want a helmet that doesn't move
around on your head when you move.

If you have a bike helmet, or a skiing or snowboarding
helmet, those are also great for skating.

Tighten the strap so that the helmet doesn't
move around on your head, but make
sure you can still open your mouth!

Getting Started
SAFETY GEAR: WRIST GUARDS

The two wristguards are not the same: one is for your right hand, and the other is for your left hand. Many people get them mixed up in the beginning!

First find the plastic side of the wrist guard. This is what you will fall onto, so that will go on the palm of your hand. Next, find the thumb hole in each wrist guard to work out which hand it should go on.

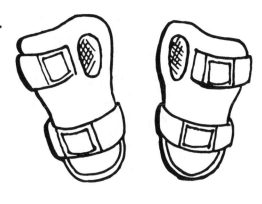

The wrist guards usually bend your wrists backward a little, so they are comfortable for falling onto.

Getting Started
SAFETY GEAR: KNEE PADS

Your knee pads are your biggest pads.
Make sure you put them on the right way up!

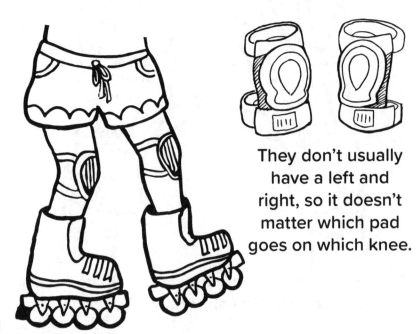

They don't usually
have a left and
right, so it doesn't
matter which pad
goes on which knee.

SAFETY GEAR: ELBOW PADS

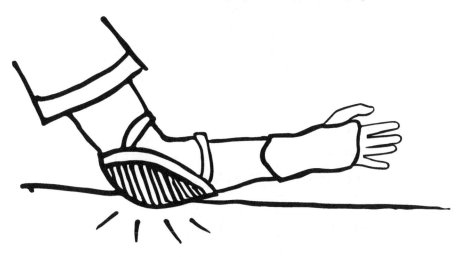

Your elbow pads look like smaller knee pads.

Make sure they're also the right way up!

Getting Started
Balance

Skating balance is like riding your bike: Once you have it, you never lose it!

We learn balance fastest by falling! So enjoy your falls instead of holding onto someone!

Fall

No Fall

Getting Started
BALANCE

When you first put your skates on, try walking around on a carpet or grass so that the wheels don't roll as easily.

Try marching on the spot to help learn to balance on your skates. See how high you can get your feet off the ground!

Getting Started
Using Cones

Most of the tricks in
this book use cones.

You don't need to use the special
skating cones from your skate
shop. You can use anything that
you don't mind falling onto and
won't get stuck in your wheels.

Upside down picnic cups
are great. You can also use
chalk. Or even pine cones!

Getting Started
Using Cones

You can put the cones
any distance apart.

For beginners, 120cm (48 inches)
is usually easiest for most tricks.

No need to measure, just use your
shoes! 120cm is about 4, 5 or 6
shoes depending on your size.

It isn't important to measure
exactly, you just want a similar
distance between all the cones.

If you have seen videos of skaters
using cones for 'slalom skating', they
are usually 80cm (32 inches) apart, or
sometimes 120cm (48 inches) apart.

TRICK LIST

		Difficulty	Genre
1	1-Foot Weave	1	Weaving
2	2-Foot Weave	1	Weaving
3	Figure 8	1	Figure 8s
4	Half Lemon Drop	1	Bubbles
5	Lemon Drop	2	Weaving
6	Lemons	2	Bubbles
7	Backward 1-Foot Weave	2	Bubbles
8	Heel Roll	3	Weaving
9	Toe Roll	3	Weaving
10	Backward 2-Foot Weave	3	Weaving
11	Backward Lemons	3	Bubbles
12	Skate Cross	3	Crosses
13	Heel Toe Roll	4	Weaving
14	Figure 8 Heel Roll	4	Figure 8s
15	Criss Cross	4	Crosses
16	Backward Skate Cross	4	Crosses
17	1 Foot Glides	4	Kicking
18	Sausage	5	Crosses
19	Backward Criss Cross	5	Crosses
20	Backward Sausage	5	Crosses

1 1-FOOT WEAVE

WHAT To Do: Skate along the line of cones and make one of your feet weave in and out of the cones. Then repeat using the other foot.

TODAY'S LESSON:
1-ft Weave

Number of Cones Needed: **5 or more in a line**

TIPS ⇨ It's easier if you get some speed before you reach the cones.

1-FOOT WEAVE

TRIES

Great Job!
5 More Tries!

PUSH YOURSELF

See if you can make your
non-weaving foot travel
in a straight line.

Color the big stars
if you make it!

 GOLD STANDARD!

 Can you do it on both sides?

2 2-FOOT WEAVE

WHAT To Do: Skate up to the line of cones and weave in and out of the cones using both feet together.

TODAY'S LESSON:
2-ft Weave

Number of Cones Needed: **5 or more in a line**

⇨ If you push one foot in front of the other, so that the feet look like train carriages, you can glide through the cones.

2-FOOT WEAVE

DIFFICULTY: 1

TRIES

Great Job!
5 More Tries!

PUSH YOURSELF

See how fast you
can weave through
the cones!

GOLD STANDARD!

Can you weave through 10
cones without ever picking
your feet off the ground?

3 FIGURE 8

WHAT To Do: Skate around the cones in a figure of 8. You'll skate around one cone clockwise, and then the next cone the other way. Then repeat.

TODAY's LESSON:
FIGURE 8

Number of Cones Needed: **Just 2, far apart**

TIPS

⇨ Pushing one foot in front of the other will help you to glide around each cone.

⇨ You may want to set up 3 cones, and then take the middle cone out. That is where you cross.

FIGURE 8

TRIES

Great Job!
5 More Tries!

(1) (2) (3) (4) (5)

(6) (7) (8) (9) (10)

PUSH YOURSELF

See how far around each
cone you can glide before
needing to skate.

GOLD STANDARD!

Can you glide without taking
any steps or pushes while
you circle each cone?

    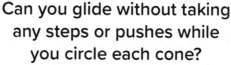

4 HALF LEMON DROP

WHAT TO DO: Start with your feet in a V with your heels together. Push your feet apart and you will roll forward. The challenge is to see if you can roll forwards and get your toes to touch each other.

TODAY'S LESSON:
Half Lemon Drop

Number of Cones Needed: **Just 1 cone**

TIPS
⇨ Press down on your big toes to help them come together to touch.
⇨ Try leaning your feet in towards each other like this:

HALF LEMON DROP

TRIES

Great Job!
5 More Tries!

PUSH YOURSELF

See how big and round you can
make your half lemon drop.

GOLD STANDARD!

Can you let yourself
roll a little backward
after the toe touch?

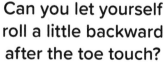

Parent/Instructor Score Sheet			Difficulty 1
Trick Number and Name	**Tried It**	**Can Do It**	**Gold Standard**
1 1-Foot Weave	Date:	Date:	Date:
2 2-Foot Weave	Date:	Date:	Date:
3 Figure 8	Date:	Date:	Date:
4 Half Lemon Drop	Date:	Date:	Date:

5 LEMON DROP

DIFFICULTY: 2

WHAT TO DO: Start with your feet in a V with your heels together. Push with your heels to roll forward and do the Half Lemon Drop. Once your toes have touched, push with your toes to roll backward until your heels touch. Keep going back and forth, touching your toes, heels, toes, heels...

TODAY'S LESSON: Lemon Drop

Number of Cones Needed: **Just 1 cone**

TIPS

⇨ When your toes are touching, bend your knees and then push your toes out. This will help you to move back to the beginning point again.

TRIES

Great Job!
5 More Tries!

DIFFICULTY: 2

PUSH YOURSELF

See how big and round you can make your Lemon Drop when going both forward and backward.

GOLD STANDARD!

Can you go back and forth, touching toes and heels 10 times in a row without missing any touches?

6 LEMONS

WHAT To Do: Do the Half Lemon Drop around the first cone. Then do another Half Lemon Drop around the second cone. Continue doing Half Lemon Drops around the rest of the cones.

TODAY'S LESSON:
Lemons

TOUCH! TOUCH! TOUCH! TOUCH!

Number of Cones Needed: **5 or more in a line**

TIPS

⇨ If you touch the sides of your skates instead of your toes, your skates can continue rolling for the whole time.

LEMONS

6

TRIES

 Great Job!
5 More Tries!

PUSH YOURSELF

How many can you do in a row?

---

*Color the big stars
if you make it!* **GOLD
STANDARD!**

Can you touch your
skates together in
between every cone?

7

BACKWARD 1-FOOT WEAVE

WHAT To Do: This is the same as the 1-Foot Weave (Trick 1), but backwards. Travel backwards along the line of cones, with one foot rolling along the cone line, and the other foot weaving in and out of the cones.

TODAY'S LESSON:
Backward
1-foot weave

Number of Cones Needed: **5 or more in a line**

TIPS ⇨ It's easier to get going if you start with the Lemon Drop (Trick 5) on the first cone.

BACKWARD 1-FOOT WEAVE

7

TRIES

*Great Job!
5 More Tries!*

① ② ③ ④ ⑤

⑥ ⑦ ⑧ ⑨ ⑩

DIFFICULTY: 2

PUSH YOURSELF

See if you can do it without
picking up either foot.

  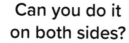

GOLD STANDARD!

Can you do it
on both sides?

Parent/Instructor Score Sheet		Difficulty 2	

Trick Number and Name	Tried It	Can Do It	Gold Standard
5 Lemon Drop	Date:	Date:	Date:
6 Lemons	Date:	Date:	Date:
7 Backward 1-Foot Weave	Date:	Date:	Date:

8   HEEL ROLL

WHAT To Do: Roll next to the line of cones. Lift one skate up onto the heel wheel and roll next to the line.

Number of Cones Needed: **5 or more in a line**

 TIPS ⇨ This is easier if you push your heel as far in front of you as you can.

HEEL ROLL

TRIES

Great Job!
5 More Tries!

PUSH YOURSELF

See how many cones you can
roll by before you need to put
the skate back down.

DIFFICULTY: 3

GOLD STANDARD!

Can you do it while
weaving in and
out of the cones?

9 TOE ROLL

WHAT To Do: Roll next to a line of cones. Lift one skate up onto the toe wheel and roll next to the line.

TODAY'S LESSON:
Toe Roll

Number of Cones Needed: **5 or more in a line**

TIPS

⇨ Put your hands onto the leg that is not on the toe.

⇨ This is easier if you push your toe as far behind you as you can.

TOE ROLL

TRIES

 Great Job!
5 More Tries!

 1   2   3   4   5

 6   7   8   9 10

DIFFICULTY: 3

PUSH YOURSELF

See how many cones you can roll by before you need to put the skate back down.

GOLD STANDARD!

Can you do it while weaving in and out of the cones?

    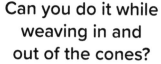

10 BACKWARD 2-FOOT WEAVE

WHAT To Do: Skate backward along the line of cones. Weave in and out of the cones as you keep moving backward.

TODAY'S LESSON:
Backward
2-foot Weave

DIFFICULTY: 3

Number of Cones Needed: **5 or more in a line**

TIPS ⇨ **Look behind you.**

BACKWARD 2-FOOT WEAVE

TRIES

10

Great Job!
5 More Tries!

1   2   3   4   5

6   7   8   9   10

PUSH YOURSELF

See if you can do only one push
for each cone that you pass.

DIFFICULTY: 3

GOLD STANDARD!

Can you do it without
picking up your feet?

11 BACKWARD LEMONS

WHAT To Do: Stand with your back to the cones and put your skates in an upside down V (toes together). Do the Half Lemon Drop backward around each cone.

DIFFICULTY: 3

Number of Cones Needed: **5 or more in a line**

TIPS

⇨ If you touch the sides of your skates instead of your heels, your skates can continue rolling for the whole time.

BACKWARD LEMONS

TRIES

Great Job!
5 More Tries!

DIFFICULTY: 3

PUSH YOURSELF

How many can you do
in a row?

GOLD STANDARD!

Can you touch your skates
together in between
every cone?

12 SKATE CROSS

What To Do: This trick is like the Half Lemon Drop except that when your toes come together, let your feet cross, one in front of the other, instead of touching your toes together.

TODAY'S LESSON:
Skate Cross

Number of Cones Needed: 2 cones

⇨ Press down on only one of your big toes so that one of your skates crosses in front of the other.

⇨ For your feet to cross, they'll need to be leaning away from each other like this:

⇨ If you need extra help, get someone to hold your hand while your feet cross.

SKATE CROSS

TRIES

Great Job! 5 More Tries!

 1
 2
 3
 4
 5

 6
 7
 8
 9
 10

DIFFICULTY: 3

PUSH YOURSELF

How far can you roll with
your legs crossed? Can you
roll fully over the cone?

GOLD STANDARD!

Can you keep rolling
and then uncross again?
If you can, then you're
GOLD STANDARD!

Parent/Instructor Score Sheet		Difficulty 3	
Trick Number and Name	Tried It	Can Do It	Gold Standard
8 Heel Roll	Date:	Date:	Date:
9 Toe Roll	Date:	Date:	Date:
10 Backward 2-Foot Weave	Date:	Date:	Date:
11 Backward Lemons	Date:	Date:	Date:
12 Skate Cross	Date:	Date:	Date:

13 HEEL-TOE ROLL

WHAT
To Do: Roll next to a line of cones. When you
reach the first cone, lift one skate up
onto the heel, and then at the next
cone, lift the other skate up onto the
toe. Keep rolling along the line of cones
in this position, with your front skate on
its heel and your back skate on its toe.

TODAY'S LESSON:
Heel-Toe Roll

DIFFICULTY: 4

Number of Cones Needed: **5 or more in a line**

 TIPS ⇨ For this trick, straight legs help!

HEEL-TOE ROLL 13

TRIES

Great Job!
5 More Tries!

 1 2 3 4 5

 6 7 8 9 10

PUSH YOURSELF

See how many cones you can
roll by before you need to put
the skates back down.

DIFFICULTY: 4

 GOLD
STANDARD!

  Can you do it while
weaving in and
out of the cones?

14 FIGURE 8 HEEL ROLL

What To Do: This trick is the same as The Figure 8, except that as you roll around each cone, you'll put the skate that is closest to the cone up onto its heel wheel. You can skate from cone to cone. As you make the cross you change to the other foot and roll on that heel wheel.

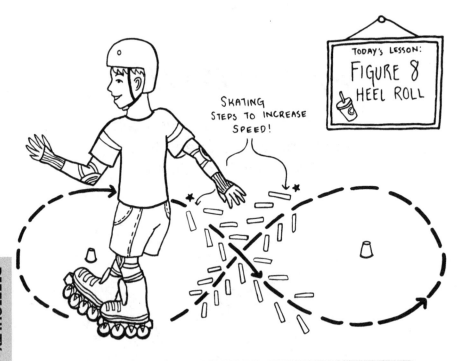

SKATING STEPS TO INCREASE SPEED!

TODAY'S LESSON: FIGURE 8 HEEL ROLL

Number of Cones Needed: **Just 2 cones, far apart**

TIPS ⇨ This is easier if you push your heel as far in front of you as you can.

FIGURE 8 HEEL ROLL

TRIES

14

Great Job! 5 More Tries!

1   2   3   4   5

6   7   8   9   10

PUSH YOURSELF

See how far around each cone you can go with your skate on the heel wheel.

GOLD STANDARD!

Can you do this with the heel wheeling foot leaning towards  the cone?

DIFFICULTY: 4

15 CRISS CROSS

WHAT To Do: This trick is the Skate Cross repeated again and again along the line of cones. So start with a Half Lemon Drop then cross your feet, then uncross and do another Half Lemon Drop, then cross... and so on.

TODAY'S LESSON:
Criss Cross

Number of Cones Needed: **5 or more in a line**

TIPS

⇨ This is easiest if you keep your feet leaning away from each other like this:

⇨ Try putting your hands on your front leg when you want to cross, and your back leg when you want to uncross.

TRIES

Great Job!
5 More Tries!

PUSH YOURSELF

Can you keep your wheels
on the ground the entire time,
even when uncrossing?

GOLD STANDARD!

Can you do it with
the other foot
crossing in front?

DIFFICULTY: 4

16 BACKWARD SKATE CROSS

WHAT To Do: This trick is like doing the Half Lemon Drop backward except that when your heels come together, let one cross in front of the other instead of touching.

TODAY'S LESSON:
Backward
Skate Cross

Number of Cones Needed: 2

DIFFICULTY: 4

TIPS

⇨ For your feet to cross, they'll need to be leaning away from each other like this:

⇨ Get someone to hold your hand while your feet cross if you need extra help.

TRIES

Great Job!
5 More Tries!

1   2   3   4   5

6   7   8   9   10

PUSH YOURSELF

How far can you roll with
your legs crossed?

Can you roll fully over the cone?

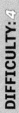

DIFFICULTY: 4

 *GOLD STANDARD!*

Can you keep rolling and
then uncross again?
If you can, then you're
GOLD STANDARD!

17   I FOOT GLIDE

WHAT To Do: Skate up to the cones and lift up one foot. See how far you can weave through the cones on only one foot!

TODAY'S LESSON:
1-foot Glide

Number of Cones Needed: **5 or more in a line**

TIPS

⇨ More speed helps.

⇨ If you put the cones closer together, you can switch directions by "hopping" from left to right.

1 FOOT GLIDE 17

TRIES

Great Job!
5 More Tries!

PUSH YOURSELF

How many cones can you roll through before putting your other foot down?

GOLD STANDARD!

Can you weave through 5 cones?
If you can, then you're
GOLD STANDARD!

Parent/Instructor Score Sheet		**Difficulty 4**	

Trick Number and Name	Tried It	Can Do It	Gold Standard
13 Heel Toe Roll	Date:	Date:	Date:
14 Figure 8 Heel Roll	Date:	Date:	Date:
15 Criss Cross	Date:	Date:	Date:
16 Backward Skate Cross	Date:	Date:	Date:
17 1 Foot Glide	Date:	Date:	Date:

18   SAUSAGE

WHAT To Do: Begin the same as you did for the Skate Cross but this time see if you can freeze in the crossed-legs position and roll until you pass an extra cone (cone 3) before uncrossing.

TODAY'S LESSON:
Sausage

Number of Cones Needed: **5 or more in a line**

TIPS

⇨ You'll need some speed for this one, so skate up to the cones.

⇨ When your feet cross, keep the weight on the front foot, or on both feet, until you want to uncross. Then lean onto the back foot.

SAUSAGE

TRIES

PUSH YOURSELF

See how many cones you
can cross before uncrossing.
How many can you do?

GOLD STANDARD!

Can you do it with the other
foot crossing in front?
If you can, then you're
GOLD STANDARD!

19 BACKWARD CRISS CROSS

WHAT To Do: This trick is the Backward Skate Cross followed by the Half Lemon Drop backward followed by the Backward Skate Cross... repeating as many times as you can.

TODAY'S LESSON:
Backward
Criss Cross

Number of Cones Needed: **5 or more in a line**

➪ This is easiest if you keep your feet leaning away from each other like this:

BACKWARD CRISS CROSS

19

TRIES

Great Job!
5 More Tries!

1   2   3   4   5

6   7   8   9   10

PUSH YOURSELF

Can you keep your wheels on
the ground the entire time,
even when uncrossing?

GOLD STANDARD!

Can you do it with
the other foot
crossing behind?

DIFFICULTY: 5

20 BACKWARD SAUSAGE

WHAT To Do: Begin the same as you did for the Backward Skate Cross but this time see if you can freeze in the crossed-legs position and roll until you pass an extra cone (cone 3) before uncrossing.

TODAY'S LESSON:
Backward
Sausage

Number of Cones Needed: **5 or more in a line**

TIPS

⇨ You'll need some speed for this one, so make sure you either start with your toes together for a big push, or start by skating up backward to the cones.

TRIES

*Great Job!
5 More Tries!*

PUSH YOURSELF

See how many cones you
can cross before uncrossing.
How many can you do?

GOLD
STANDARD!

Can you do it with
the other foot
crossing in behind?

DIFFICULTY: 5

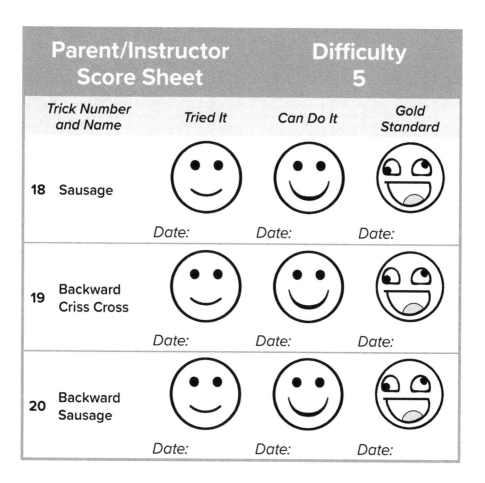

Trick Number and Name	Tried It	Can Do It	Gold Standard
18 Sausage	Date:	Date:	Date:
19 Backward Criss Cross	Date:	Date:	Date:
20 Backward Sausage	Date:	Date:	Date:

Parent/Instructor Score Sheet

Difficulty 5